MAYER SMITH

The Billionaire's Secret Garden

Copyright © 2025 by Mayer Smith

All rights reserved. No part of this publication may be reproduced, stored or transmitted in any form or by any means, electronic, mechanical, photocopying, recording, scanning, or otherwise without written permission from the publisher. It is illegal to copy this book, post it to a website, or distribute it by any other means without permission.

This novel is entirely a work of fiction. The names, characters and incidents portrayed in it are the work of the author's imagination. Any resemblance to actual persons, living or dead, events or localities is entirely coincidental.

Mayer Smith asserts the moral right to be identified as the author of this work.

Mayer Smith has no responsibility for the persistence or accuracy of URLs for external or third-party Internet Websites referred to in this publication and does not guarantee that any content on such Websites is, or will remain, accurate or appropriate.

Designations used by companies to distinguish their products are often claimed as trademarks. All brand names and product names used in this book and on its cover are trade names, service marks, trademarks and registered trademarks of their respective owners. The publishers and the book are not associated with any product or vendor mentioned in this book. None of the companies referenced within the book have endorsed the book.

First edition

*This book was professionally typeset on Reedsy.
Find out more at reedsy.com*

Contents

1	A New Beginning	1
2	The First Encounter	8
3	Unmasking the Past	15
4	Blossoms of Friendship	21
5	A Seed of Attraction	27
6	Secrets in the Garden	33
7	The Unraveling	40
8	Fractured Trust	46
9	Healing Wounds	52
10	Blooming Together	58

One

A New Beginning

The small town of Greenvale was a world of its own, nestled in the rolling hills and green meadows that seemed to stretch forever in every direction. It was the kind of place where everyone knew everyone, where news traveled faster than the morning sun could rise. It was the kind of place Samantha had never belonged to—or so she thought.

She stood at the window of her modest second-floor apartment above the little flower shop she had just opened. Outside, the sun was setting, casting an orange glow across the town's cobblestone streets. There was something about the peacefulness of the scene that appealed to her, something that made her feel as though this quiet town was exactly what she needed. Here, she wasn't the daughter of a billionaire or a renowned botanist. Here, she was Sarah, the simple florist with a love for flowers and a desire to escape the chaos of her old life.

The Billionaire's Secret Garden

A deep breath filled her lungs as she closed her eyes, letting the calmness wash over her. This was the beginning of something new. No one knew her here. No one had any expectations. She had shed the heavy burden of being someone she wasn't, and for the first time in a long while, she felt free.

The bell above the door jingled, snapping her from her reverie. She turned, her heart skipping a beat, unsure of who might be walking in. It was late in the evening, and most of the customers had already left for the day. Still, the shop was open, and she welcomed anyone who sought comfort in the blooms she lovingly arranged.

A man stepped through the door, his rugged appearance immediately catching her attention. He was tall, with broad shoulders that hinted at a life lived outside of a desk. His face was framed by a short, scruffy beard, and his eyes—eyes that seemed to hold a thousand untold stories—locked onto hers with quiet intensity. His clothes were simple but practical: a well-worn leather jacket, faded jeans, and sturdy boots that spoke of someone used to hard work.

"Evening," the man said with a slight smile, his voice low and gravelly.

Samantha nodded, offering a polite smile in return. "Good evening. How can I help you?"

He glanced around the shop, taking in the rows of vibrant flowers and the sweet scent that seemed to cling to every surface. "It's a beautiful place you have here," he remarked, his voice softening as he surveyed the colorful arrangements. "I'm just passing through, but I couldn't help but stop."

"Thank you," she said, a little surprised by the compliment. "I've only just opened. I've always loved flowers."

The man nodded thoughtfully. "You can tell. The way you've arranged everything... it's like you're speaking to the plants, not just selling them."

His words caught her off guard. Most people saw flowers as just a product, a thing to buy and use for a brief moment. But to her, they were much more than that—they were life, a language all their own. "I believe they speak to us, if we're willing to listen," she said quietly, almost to herself.

The man seemed to notice the change in her tone. His eyes softened, and he stepped closer to the counter where a bouquet of roses sat, their red petals dark and velvety. "I think I'd like a bouquet for my daughter. It's her birthday tomorrow."

Samantha's heart warmed at the mention of a child. There was something about children that always brought out a protective instinct in her, even though she had never had any of her own. "What kind of flowers does she like?" she asked, moving toward him.

"Daisies," the man said, a slight chuckle escaping his lips. "She's always liked daisies. I don't know what it is about them, but she loves them."

The Billionaire's Secret Garden

Samantha smiled, reaching for a bunch of fresh daisies that were perfectly arranged in a vase. She could already picture the way they would brighten up a room, their white petals contrasting with the deep green of their stems. "I'll make a special arrangement for her."

He watched her work, his gaze lingering on her hands as she expertly combined the daisies with other flowers—soft pink peonies, lavender sprigs, and a few delicate lilies. There was an artistry to the way she moved, a grace that made the simple act of flower arranging seem almost magical. It was a gift, one that she had perfected over the years, but it was also a way for her to escape the overwhelming demands of her previous life. The delicate balance of creating something beautiful out of nature's simplest gifts was her own form of therapy.

As she finished the bouquet, she handed it to him with a soft smile. "Here you go. I hope she loves it."

The man took the flowers, his fingers brushing against hers for the briefest moment. It was nothing more than a fleeting touch, but the warmth of it lingered. His eyes met hers, and for a moment, neither of them spoke. The world outside the shop seemed to quiet, as if the very air was holding its breath.

"Thank you," he said softly, his voice betraying a hint of vulnerability. "You've done something beautiful here."

Samantha nodded, unsure of how to respond. "I'm glad you like it."

A New Beginning

He hesitated for a moment, his hand on the door handle, but then he looked back at her. "I'm Alex," he said, offering a smile that didn't quite reach his eyes. "I'll be back. I've got a feeling that this place is special."

"Sarah," she replied, her voice barely above a whisper. "I'll be here."

With that, he stepped out into the evening, the door closing softly behind him. Samantha stood still for a moment, her fingers still tingling from the brief contact. She shook her head, trying to rid herself of the strange feeling that had settled in her chest.

It was a feeling she couldn't quite name—a mix of warmth and curiosity. Something about Alex had triggered something inside her, something she hadn't felt in a long time. But she quickly pushed the thought away. This was her new life, and she needed to focus on that. No distractions. No complications.

The sound of her phone vibrating on the counter broke her from her thoughts. She picked it up, her heart sinking as she saw the name on the screen.

Her father.

Taking a deep breath, she swiped to answer the call. "Hello?"

"Samantha," her father's voice came through, sharp and commanding as ever. "Where are you? Your mother and I are waiting for you. We need to discuss your future, your responsibilities. The board is calling for a meeting, and they want you to attend."

"I can't," she said quietly, her grip tightening on the phone. "I'm not coming back. I've found a place for myself here."

"Don't be ridiculous," he snapped. "You can't hide away forever. You're needed here. You have a position to uphold."

Samantha closed her eyes, a pang of guilt coursing through her. "I'm not hiding. I'm just… trying to find myself."

Her father's silence on the other end of the line was deafening. "You'll regret this," he finally said, his voice cold. "But if that's what you want, fine. Don't come crawling back when it all falls apart."

The line went dead, and she stood there, holding the phone in her trembling hand. For a moment, she allowed herself to feel the weight of it—the overwhelming pressure of being someone she wasn't. But then, as the sound of the town outside her window drifted back into her ears, she made a decision. She wasn't going back. Not now, not ever.

With a deep breath, she placed the phone down and walked over to the window, looking out into the fading twilight. This was her chance at a new beginning, and she wasn't going to let anyone take it away from her.

Outside, the town of Greenvale hummed with life. But inside her little flower shop, a new chapter was about to unfold—one that would change everything.

And for the first time in a long time, Samantha felt like she was exactly where she was meant to be.

Two

The First Encounter

The little town of Greenvale was beginning to feel like home, though Samantha knew it wasn't quite there yet. She had settled in quickly enough, her life as "Sarah" taking root in the small flower shop she had opened in the heart of the town. The quaint streets, the rows of local shops, and the warmth of the people had all become familiar to her. But despite the town's charm, a part of her remained aloof, cautious. She couldn't afford to get too comfortable, not yet.

Samantha spent her mornings arranging flowers, keeping the shop's vibrant displays in order. She loved the peace of it— the hum of the town outside her door, the quiet beauty of the blooms she tended to. Each petal she carefully placed in a bouquet felt like a small act of rebellion against the life she had left behind, the life of wealth, expectations, and constant surveillance. Here, in the small, dusty town of Greenvale, she

The First Encounter

was just Sarah. A woman with a modest flower shop and no history to hide.

It was the afternoon when he walked in. The bell above the door jingled, pulling Samantha's attention away from the display of hydrangeas she had been fussing over. She looked up, and for a moment, the world seemed to pause. Standing in the doorway was a man, tall and broad-shouldered, wearing a weathered leather jacket and jeans that looked like they had seen their fair share of hard work. His hair was dark, a little tousled, and his eyes—dark and intense—met hers as if he had been searching for her without knowing it.

Samantha's heart skipped a beat, and she quickly looked down, trying to mask the sudden flutter of nerves in her stomach. She was not one to feel this way—at least, she hadn't allowed herself to feel this way in years. She was Sarah, remember? Just Sarah. A florist. No distractions. No complications.

But there he was, a living, breathing complication. And for some reason, something in her chest tightened.

"Afternoon," the man said, his voice low and gravelly, but with a warmth that seemed to seep into the room. "I'm looking for something special for my daughter's birthday. She's a big fan of flowers."

Samantha nodded, trying to push the sudden nervousness away. "Of course," she replied, forcing a smile. "I'd be happy to help."

He walked into the shop fully, his presence filling the space in a way that felt strangely overwhelming. There was something about him that felt… different. He didn't belong here, not in the way she did, yet there was a kind of ease about him, a quiet confidence that seemed to fit right in.

"I'm Alex," he said as he approached the counter, a slight chuckle in his voice. "And I'm afraid I don't know much about flowers. I'm hoping you can help me pick something out."

Samantha smiled softly. "You've come to the right place. What kind of flowers does your daughter like?"

"Daisies, I think," he said, a touch of uncertainty in his voice. "She's always liked daisies, for some reason. I don't know why, but she says they make her happy."

"That's sweet," Samantha said, her heart softening at the thought of a father caring so much about what his daughter loved. "We can do something with daisies, but we can mix them with some other blooms, make it a little more interesting. Something that would stand out."

"Sounds perfect," Alex said, his gaze lingering on her for a moment longer than was necessary, his expression thoughtful. Samantha turned away, her cheeks heating slightly. She could feel his eyes on her, and the moment stretched out longer than she was comfortable with.

As she began to pick the daisies from the cooler and arrange them with the other flowers, she couldn't help but steal a glance back at him. Alex was standing by the counter now, his hands

The First Encounter

tucked into his pockets, his brow furrowed as he watched her work. She noticed that he was deep in thought, almost as if he were studying her.

Samantha found herself hesitating as she worked, her fingers brushing the petals more carefully than they probably needed to be. She couldn't quite explain why, but something about him felt... different. Maybe it was the way he looked at her, as if he saw more than just a florist behind the counter. Or maybe it was the way his presence seemed to fill the room, as if he wasn't just standing there, but taking in everything, paying attention to every detail. Samantha had spent years being watched, being scrutinized by people who only saw her as the heir to a fortune. It was the last thing she wanted now, but with Alex, she didn't feel quite so exposed. His gaze wasn't judgmental; it was... interested. Curious.

"I've never really been good with flowers," Alex said, breaking her reverie. "But I like the way they make people feel. The way they seem to bring life to a place."

She smiled, looking up at him. "I think that's the magic of flowers. They bring something else to a room—something alive, something that can't be replaced. They speak in ways words can't."

"Yeah," he agreed quietly, his eyes meeting hers for a moment. Then, as though he were pulling himself out of a thought, he added, "I guess that's why I thought this shop would be a good place for her."

The Billionaire's Secret Garden

Samantha nodded, finishing the arrangement and placing it carefully on the counter. "Here you go. I think these will be perfect for her."

Alex reached for the bouquet, taking in the bright colors and the gentle arrangement of flowers. He smiled, a real, genuine smile that softened his usually serious expression. "I think she'll love it. Thank you."

"Of course," Samantha said, feeling a strange flutter in her chest at his smile. "It's always a pleasure to make something special for someone."

There was a moment of silence between them, and Samantha couldn't help but feel that the air had shifted in some way. Maybe it was just her, but something about Alex seemed different—like he wasn't just a passing customer. He lingered, in the way he looked at her, the way he spoke. He wasn't like the other men who had come through the shop in the past, making small talk about arrangements, paying and leaving without a second thought. Alex was… different.

"You know, I was thinking," he said suddenly, his voice soft but with an edge of something she couldn't quite place. "This shop of yours… it's not just a shop, is it? It's more than that."

Samantha looked up, startled. She hadn't expected him to pick up on that. She hadn't even consciously been aware of it herself. But now, with his words hanging in the air, she realized that maybe it wasn't just the flowers that made her love this place. Maybe it was the way it felt like a safe haven, a place where she could escape the life that had been imposed upon her.

"I suppose you could say that," she replied, trying to keep her voice neutral. "I didn't come here just to sell flowers."

Alex didn't respond right away. He only nodded, as if mulling over her words. He looked at her again, his expression unreadable. For a moment, it seemed as though he was about to say something else, something deeper, but then he just took a step back, his shoulders relaxing.

"I'll take it," he said finally, his voice casual but with an underlying warmth. "Thank you, Sarah. For this. And for listening."

Samantha blinked, unsure of what he meant by listening, but before she could ask, he had already turned toward the door. The soft jingle of the bell echoed through the shop, and just like that, he was gone.

She stood there for a long moment, staring at the door as it slowly swung closed behind him. Her fingers still tingled from where she had touched the bouquet, and something unfamiliar and unsettling twisted in her stomach. She wasn't sure what it was—whether it was the lingering warmth of Alex's presence or the feeling that he had seen something in her that no one else had ever bothered to look for.

Whatever it was, it had unsettled her, in a way she wasn't sure she was ready to confront.

She didn't know when it had happened, but she knew one thing for sure: something had shifted. And whatever it was, it was pulling her toward Alex in a way she wasn't sure she could resist.

Three

Unmasking the Past

Samantha sat alone in the dim light of her flower shop, the last rays of the setting sun filtering through the windows and casting long shadows across the room. The stillness of the evening was a sharp contrast to the swirling thoughts in her mind. She had come to Greenvale to escape her past, to live a life where her name wasn't synonymous with wealth and expectations. She had wanted peace, simplicity, and the anonymity that this small town promised. But as the days passed, it became increasingly clear that escaping her past was more difficult than she had imagined.

Her phone sat on the counter in front of her, vibrating relentlessly, the screen lighting up with each call from her father. She hadn't answered a single one. He had been relentless, urging her to return home, reminding her of her responsibilities—both to the family and the business. She had never wanted any part of that life, the life of parties and board meetings, the endless charades of wealth and status. But her father's voice, with its commanding tone, had always found its way into her conscience, reminding her that there was no escaping who she was. No escaping what they expected her to be.

Samantha picked up the phone, her fingers trembling as she slid it open to read the latest message.

"Sarah, it's time to come home. Your presence is required. The board is calling. They want you to take over. Do not make me repeat myself."

Her breath caught in her throat. The board. The family business. She had done everything she could to stay away from it. But they were persistent. Relentless. And now, it seemed, they had found her—once again, she was being dragged back into a world she wanted nothing to do with.

The bell above the door jingled, breaking her out of her trance. She quickly put the phone down, wiping her hands on her apron as she turned to face the entrance. Alex stood in the doorway, his silhouette framed by the golden light of the evening. For a moment, their eyes met, and something in the air shifted. There was a new tension between them, a subtle charge that hadn't been there the first time he had walked in.

"Evening," he said, his voice softer than usual, as though he too felt the weight of the moment.

"Evening," Samantha replied, her voice betraying the unease that bubbled beneath the surface. She hadn't expected him to return, not so soon. Not after the way things had ended between them the other day.

Alex stepped inside, the door clicking shut behind him. His gaze swept across the room, lingering on the flowers and the peaceful arrangement she had worked so hard to cultivate. But there was something else in his eyes now—something more than the casual interest of a customer. It was as though he could see through the layers of her carefully constructed façade, as if he knew there was more to her than the quiet florist standing before him.

"I... I was hoping to speak with you," Alex said, his voice steady but with an underlying hint of concern.

Samantha nodded, motioning to the counter. "Sure, of course. What's on your mind?"

He hesitated for a moment, his eyes scanning her face as if trying to read something she wasn't saying. Then, with a sigh, he crossed the room and set a small envelope down on the counter in front of her. The paper was thick and cream-colored, the kind that only came from places with too much money to care about using anything else. Samantha's heart skipped a beat.

"What's this?" she asked, her fingers tracing the edge of the envelope. The handwriting on the front was unmistakable—her father's. She had seen it a thousand times before, on letters, contracts, and board meeting agendas.

"I didn't know if I should give this to you," Alex said, his voice quiet but insistent. "But when I went to the post office today, they told me this was addressed to you. It came in the morning, but... I figured you didn't want to be bothered by it. But now..." He trailed off, glancing at her with a look that mixed concern with confusion.

Samantha's throat tightened. She reached for the envelope, the weight of it in her hands feeling almost too heavy to bear. Her fingers shook slightly as she tore it open, the sound of the paper pulling apart too loud in the silence of the room.

Inside was a single letter. She recognized the embossed seal on the top immediately—it was from her family's estate. The letter was short, direct, and to the point.

"Sarah, the time has come. You are needed back at the helm of the company. There is no further excuse for you to hide away. Your responsibilities await. Do not test our patience."

Her father's words, cold and unyielding, sent a wave of panic through her chest. Her past was catching up to her. There was no running from it. The letter felt like a chain, binding her to the life she had so desperately tried to escape.

Alex watched her, his face a mixture of understanding and concern. "I... I don't know what's going on, but I can see it's affecting you. You don't have to explain it to me. But I want you to know, you don't have to go back there. Not if you don't want to."

Samantha looked up at him, her eyes filled with a mixture of gratitude and something else—something she hadn't quite allowed herself to acknowledge until now. She had come to care for Alex more than she had ever intended. He wasn't just a distraction. He was a lifeline, someone who, in his own quiet way, had become a part of the world she had built here in Greenvale. A world she was now terrified of losing.

But her family's expectations were like a looming storm, and she knew there was no outrunning it. She had tried for so long to hide, to live a life free from the suffocating grip of wealth and power. But now, it seemed, they were pulling her back in.

She swallowed hard, trying to steady her breath. "I have to go back," she said quietly, her voice breaking the silence. "There's no choice. They won't stop until I do."

Alex stepped closer, his expression softening. "But why? Why let them control your life like that?"

Samantha's chest tightened as she placed the letter back in the envelope, her hands shaking. "Because… because they won't stop. They'll keep coming, and eventually, I'll lose everything I've worked for here. This life… Greenvale… it won't be enough. Not against them."

"Is that what you really want? To go back to that life?" Alex asked, his voice firm but gentle. "Because from where I'm standing, you've built something good here. Something real. Don't let them take it away from you."

The Billionaire's Secret Garden

She shook her head, the tears threatening to spill over. "I don't know if I have a choice," she whispered.

Alex didn't respond right away. Instead, he reached for the flowers she had carefully arranged on the counter earlier, his fingers grazing the soft petals. "I can't pretend to know what you're going through, Sarah. But I can tell you this—whatever happens, you're not alone. You don't have to go back and face them by yourself."

For a moment, Samantha just stared at him, the weight of his words settling deep in her chest. He was offering her something she hadn't realized she needed—a chance to choose a different path. A chance to take control, to fight back against the life she had always felt shackled to.

But the letter still burned in her hands, a reminder that her past was never truly gone. No matter how far she ran, it was always one step behind, waiting to pull her back into its grip.

And yet, as she looked at Alex, something stirred inside her. For the first time in years, she wasn't sure if she had to follow the path they had laid out for her. Maybe, just maybe, she could still make her own way.

But could she? The decision seemed impossible.

Four

Blossoms of Friendship

The days that followed the arrival of her father's letter felt like a fog that enveloped Samantha, clouding her thoughts and making the world around her seem distant and unclear. Despite Alex's quiet insistence that she didn't have to go back to her old life, the reality of her situation pressed against her like a weight she couldn't shake off. She spent long hours in the flower shop, arranging bouquets and trimming stems, her mind drifting to the letter, to her father's demand. It was as if her life in Greenvale—her new life—was hanging by a thread, one tug away from unraveling.

The shop had become her sanctuary, a place where she could lose herself in the rhythmic motions of arranging flowers, where the weight of her past could be momentarily forgotten. But even here, in the comfort of the familiar, she couldn't escape the looming tension in her chest. The more she tried to focus on her work, the more the pressure built, like the petals of a flower closing in on themselves, suffocating under the weight of their own existence.

It was just past noon on a warm spring day when Alex walked into the shop again. His presence had become a steady comfort in the days since the letter arrived, but today there was something different about him. He seemed more purposeful, more determined. His eyes were focused, yet there was a subtle vulnerability in the way he moved. It was as if he, too, was carrying something heavy, something unspoken.

"Hey, Sarah," he greeted, his voice carrying the usual warmth, but there was an underlying tension that Samantha couldn't ignore.

"Hi, Alex," she replied, trying to hide the unease she felt creeping up her spine. "What brings you in today?"

He paused for a moment, glancing around the shop as if searching for the right words. "I was hoping we could talk," he said, his eyes meeting hers with an intensity that made her heart skip a beat. "I think you've been avoiding me."

The admission caught her off guard. She had been trying to keep her distance, unwilling to let anyone in, especially Alex. She didn't want to burden him with the complexity of her life, with the secrets she was desperately trying to keep hidden. And yet, here he was, sensing her withdrawal, not letting her push him away.

"I'm sorry," she said, her voice faltering. "It's just… everything's been so complicated lately."

"I can tell," Alex said softly, his gaze never leaving hers. "But you don't have to go through it alone."

His words were simple, yet they struck something deep within her. She had spent so much time hiding, so much time thinking she could handle everything by herself, but in this moment, she realized how much she needed someone—someone who saw her for who she really was, not just the version of herself she had carefully constructed.

"I don't want to burden you with my problems," she said, her voice barely above a whisper. "You have enough on your plate already."

Alex stepped closer, the sound of his boots against the floor echoing in the quiet shop. "Sarah, you're not a burden. We're friends, aren't we? And friends help each other, no matter what."

The word "friends" lingered in the air between them, heavy and meaningful. She had never allowed herself to form true friendships before, always too guarded, too afraid of what might happen if someone found out who she really was. But with Alex, it felt different. It felt safe.

Samantha swallowed, her throat tight. "I don't know what to do anymore, Alex. I don't know if I can keep running from my past. My family… they won't stop until they get what they want."

Alex's expression softened, and he reached out, gently placing his hand on hers. His touch was warm, grounding her in the present moment. "You don't have to do it alone. Whatever decision you make, I'm here for you. You don't have to go back to that life if you don't want to."

Samantha's heart fluttered at his words, but a part of her wanted to pull away, to remind herself that this wasn't her life, that she didn't belong here. She was a stranger in this town, someone hiding from the very world that had shaped her. She wasn't the simple florist everyone thought she was. She wasn't Sarah. She was Samantha, the daughter of a billionaire, a woman bound by responsibilities and expectations she couldn't escape.

But looking into Alex's eyes, she felt a flicker of something she hadn't felt in years—hope. Maybe, just maybe, there was a way out. Maybe there was a chance for her to have the life she wanted, the life she had dreamed of since she was a little girl.

"I don't know if I'm strong enough to face them," she admitted, her voice shaky. "I don't know if I can stand up to my family, to my father."

Alex squeezed her hand, his grip reassuring. "You are stronger than you think, Sarah. And you don't have to face them alone. I'll be here, every step of the way."

For a moment, the world outside the shop seemed to fade away. The only thing that mattered was the warmth of Alex's hand in hers, the unspoken promise that they were in this together. The tension in her chest, the constant weight of her past, seemed to ease, if only for a moment. And in that moment, she allowed herself to believe that maybe, just maybe, she could find a way to make this new life her own.

As the day wore on, Samantha and Alex spent hours together in the flower shop, talking, laughing, and arranging flowers. They talked about everything and nothing at all—about their favorite flowers, about the weather, about life. It was the kind of conversation that felt natural, easy. And in it, Samantha found a sense of peace she hadn't realized she was missing.

But as the evening drew near, the reality of her situation began to settle back in. Her father's letter, the pressure of the family business, the expectations that weighed on her like a heavy cloak—it was all still there, lurking just beneath the surface, waiting to drag her back into the life she had worked so hard to escape.

Alex, sensing the shift in her mood, paused in his work and turned to face her. "You're thinking about it again, aren't you?" he asked gently.

Samantha nodded, her fingers trembling as she adjusted the petals of a bouquet. "I don't know how to escape it, Alex. I don't know how to leave that life behind and stay here. It's like the past is always chasing me."

"You don't have to outrun your past, Sarah," he said softly. "You just have to decide who you want to be. And then, you fight for that person, no matter what."

His words struck her deeply. It was so simple, yet so profound. She didn't have to outrun her past. She just had to stand her ground and fight for the future she wanted. It wasn't going to be easy, but with Alex by her side, maybe it was possible.

"Maybe… maybe I can stay," she said, the words tasting strange on her tongue. "Maybe I can build a life here, one that's just mine. But it's going to take time. And I'm scared."

Alex smiled, his eyes soft and kind. "Then we'll take it one step at a time, together."

For the first time in a long while, Samantha allowed herself to believe that maybe, just maybe, she could have the life she dreamed of. A life not defined by her past, but by her own choices. And with Alex's quiet support, perhaps she had found the strength to make that choice.

As the evening wore on, and the shop began to quiet, Samantha realized that she wasn't just planting flowers in the soil. She was planting something else—hope, friendship, and maybe even love. The seeds were small, but they were taking root, and for the first time in a long time, she felt like she had a future worth fighting for.

And maybe, just maybe, she could finally bloom.

Five

A Seed of Attraction

The air in Greenvale had grown thick with the scent of spring, and the town was blooming in every sense. The streets were lined with colorful flowers, and the town square buzzed with the hum of life as locals went about their business, going in and out of the shops that lined the cobbled streets. But for Samantha, there was only one place she cared about—the flower shop. It had become her refuge, the one place where she could be herself, away from the prying eyes of her past, away from the responsibilities she had left behind.

And yet, as much as she tried to ignore it, her thoughts kept drifting back to Alex. It had been weeks since their conversation, since he had promised to be there for her, but the weight of her past still loomed large. She didn't know how to reconcile the two parts of her life—the woman who worked in the flower shop, who was building something real in Greenvale, and the woman who was the heir to a fortune, to a legacy that she had tried so hard to escape.

She couldn't deny the attraction she felt toward Alex. It was undeniable, a force that seemed to pull her toward him with an intensity that both frightened and excited her. Every time he walked into the shop, every time their eyes met, there was an electric charge in the air, something unspoken, something neither of them had dared to acknowledge. But with every passing day, it grew harder to ignore.

She had learned to guard her emotions, to protect herself from getting too close to anyone. But with Alex, it felt different. There was no pretense with him. No facade. He was just a man—a man who had seen something in her that no one else had, someone who cared enough to fight for her, to stand by her side. He wasn't interested in the wealth, the name, or the legacy that had defined her life. He was interested in the woman who tended to the flowers, the woman who had dreams and desires of her own.

But how could she let herself fall for someone like him? A man who had no idea who she really was, who had no clue about the life she had left behind. And what would happen if he found out? Would he still look at her the same way? Would he still be the man who cared for her, or would she become just another woman caught up in the web of her family's expectations and wealth?

Her thoughts were interrupted by the familiar sound of the shop door opening. She turned, expecting to see one of the regulars, but instead, Alex stood there, his broad shoulders filling the doorway, his eyes meeting hers with that familiar intensity.

"Hey," he greeted, his voice steady but with an undercurrent of something else. Something she couldn't quite place. "Do you have a moment?"

Samantha swallowed, her heart racing. "Of course," she replied, trying to keep her voice steady. "What's going on?"

He stepped inside, closing the door behind him. There was something different about him today. Something in the way he held himself, something in his eyes. He seemed… unsettled, as if he were wrestling with something he wasn't sure how to express.

"I've been thinking," he began, his voice quiet, but urgent. "About you. About us."

Samantha's breath caught in her throat. She had been trying to keep her emotions in check, trying to keep her distance from him, but now, with him standing there, so close, so real, she could feel the pull between them stronger than ever.

"I know you've got a lot going on," Alex continued, his voice tinged with something she couldn't quite define. "But I can't stop thinking about you, Sarah. About what this… whatever this is between us, could be."

Her heart raced. She wanted to speak, to say something, but the words caught in her throat. How could she explain to him what was really going on? How could she tell him that the person he thought she was—the simple florist—was only a mask, a persona she had created to hide from the world?

"I..." she started, but she couldn't find the words. The weight of her secret felt suffocating, like a wall she couldn't break through, even though she wanted to. But how could she risk everything—her life, her freedom—by telling him the truth? How could she ask him to accept the woman she really was, with all the baggage and complications that came with it?

Alex's expression softened as he took a step closer to her. "Sarah, you don't have to say anything right now," he said, his voice gentle. "I just... I just need to know if you feel the same way."

The words hung in the air, heavy and unspoken. Samantha's heart pounded in her chest. She felt herself drawn to him, felt the longing building inside her, the need to reach out and close the distance between them. But fear held her back, fear of what it would mean if she allowed herself to fall for him. She had never let herself get this close to anyone before, and now, with Alex, she wasn't sure if she could stop herself.

She took a deep breath, her fingers trembling as she reached for the bouquet she had been working on earlier. "I do," she whispered, the words barely escaping her lips. "But I'm not sure how... how it could work."

Alex's eyes softened, and he reached out to touch her hand. "It's not about how it could work, Sarah. It's about whether we're willing to try. Together."

A Seed of Attraction

Samantha's breath caught in her throat. The intensity in his eyes, the sincerity in his voice, was enough to make her heart ache. But the fear still lingered, the fear that everything she had built—everything she had worked so hard to protect—would come crashing down if she let herself fall for him.

"I want to try," she said, her voice barely a whisper. "But I'm scared, Alex. I'm scared of what it means. What it could cost me."

Alex nodded, his grip on her hand tightening just slightly. "I can't promise you that it'll be easy, or that there won't be things you'll have to face that you don't want to. But I can promise you that I'm here for you. That I'll be here, no matter what."

The sincerity in his words, the trust he was offering her, sent a wave of emotion crashing over her. For the first time in a long time, she allowed herself to believe in the possibility of something real, something that wasn't tied to her past, to the wealth, the expectations, or the legacy she had tried so desperately to escape.

As Alex stepped closer, his hand gently cupping her face, Samantha closed her eyes, allowing herself to feel the warmth of his touch. She could feel the tension in her chest easing, the walls she had built around herself slowly crumbling. She had spent so long hiding from the world, hiding from herself, and now, for the first time in years, she was letting someone in.

She opened her eyes, meeting his gaze. "I'm scared," she whispered again, but this time, there was a sense of acceptance

The Billionaire's Secret Garden

in her voice, as if she was finally acknowledging the fear and the possibility that came with it.

"I know," Alex said softly. "But we don't have to be afraid together."

And in that moment, as their lips met in a kiss that was soft and tentative at first, but quickly deepened with the weight of everything unspoken, Samantha realized that maybe, just maybe, she wasn't as alone as she had always believed. Maybe, just maybe, Alex was the person who could help her bloom again, despite the darkness of her past.

As the kiss broke, Samantha pulled back slightly, her breath uneven, her heart racing in her chest. She knew there was still so much she had to face, so many questions that needed answering, but for the first time in a long time, she didn't feel afraid.

With Alex by her side, she could face whatever came next.

Six

Secrets in the Garden

The garden behind the flower shop was a sanctuary, a secret world of her own making. It was the one place where she could truly be herself, where she could let go of the persona she had crafted for years. The flowers in the garden, like the ones in her shop, were her creations—her quiet rebellion against the world that demanded so much of her.

Samantha had spent countless hours cultivating the garden, choosing each plant with care, each bloom a piece of her soul. Here, in this lush green space, she could forget who her family wanted her to be and simply exist. But even this place, this sanctuary, had its secrets. And for the first time in a long time, those secrets felt like they were coming for her.

The evening air was heavy with the scent of jasmine and roses, the faint hum of insects drifting through the stillness. Samantha knelt in the garden, her fingers digging into the earth as she planted a new row of tulips, her thoughts as tangled as the vines creeping along the trellis. It had been a week since the kiss with Alex, a week since she had let herself believe in something real. But the weight of her past was still there, hovering at the edges of her mind, threatening to pull her back into a world she had fought so hard to leave behind.

She wiped the sweat from her brow and stood up, surveying the garden with a sense of satisfaction. The plants were thriving, the flowers vibrant with color. But beneath the beauty, something else was growing—something darker. Her father's constant calls, the letters, the demands, had become impossible to ignore. The life she had carved out for herself in Greenvale was slipping away, one piece at a time.

"Sarah?"

The sound of Alex's voice broke through her thoughts, and she turned to see him standing at the edge of the garden, his posture hesitant but determined. She hadn't expected him to be here. She hadn't told him about the garden, hadn't invited him into this part of her world. This was her space, her escape. But here he was, standing in the doorway to the sanctuary she had tried so hard to keep to herself.

"Alex," she said, her voice softer than she intended. "What are you doing here?"

He took a step forward, his gaze never leaving hers. "I was hoping we could talk. I've been thinking about us… about you.

And I don't know if you're ready to talk about it, but I need to know what's going on."

Her heart skipped a beat, and she felt a sudden rush of heat flood her face. She had tried to keep him at arm's length, to protect herself from the vulnerability that seemed to come so easily with him. But now, standing in front of him, she couldn't hide the truth any longer.

"I don't know what you mean," she said, trying to sound casual, though her pulse raced in her ears.

"I think you do," he replied softly. "I think you've been keeping something from me. Something big. And I can see it in your eyes—whatever it is, it's tearing you apart."

Samantha swallowed, her throat tight. She hadn't realized how much she had been hiding until that moment. But Alex wasn't just any man. He was someone who could see through her carefully constructed walls, who could read her as if she were an open book. And the thought of him knowing her truth—the truth she had been running from for so long—was terrifying.

She glanced around the garden, the overgrown ivy and fragrant flowers all seeming to close in on her. This was the place she had come to in order to escape, to hide. But there was no more hiding now. No more pretending.

"Alex," she began, her voice cracking as the words tumbled out. "I… I'm not who you think I am. I'm not just Sarah, the florist in Greenvale. I'm… I'm Samantha."

The name hung in the air, a heavy truth that she had never allowed herself to speak aloud. She could see the confusion in Alex's eyes as he took a step closer, his brow furrowing in concern.

"Samantha?" he asked, his voice barely above a whisper. "What... what does that mean? Who are you?"

Samantha took a deep breath, her heart pounding in her chest. She had never intended to tell him this. She had never wanted to burden him with the weight of her past. But there was no turning back now.

"I'm the daughter of a billionaire," she said, her words tumbling out in a rush. "My family... they own a massive company. A legacy. They've been grooming me my whole life to take over, to follow in my father's footsteps. I didn't want it. I never wanted any of it. So I ran. I left it all behind."

Alex's eyes widened, and he took another step toward her, his voice rising in disbelief. "Wait. You're telling me that you're—"

"A billionaire's daughter, yes," she interrupted, her voice breaking. "I've spent my whole life hiding behind a mask. Hiding from them, hiding from what they want me to be. I moved here to get away from all of it. To live a simple life, to be someone else. But I can't outrun it. It's always there, lurking in the background. My father... he's been trying to drag me back into that world. The world I've spent years running from."

Alex stared at her, his expression a mixture of shock and

Secrets in the Garden

confusion. "So... all this time, you've been hiding who you really are? From me? From everyone?"

Samantha nodded, tears welling in her eyes. "I never wanted you to know. I never wanted anyone to know. But you've seen through me. You've seen the cracks in the mask. And now, I don't know what to do. I don't know how to keep running from them."

There was a long silence between them, the only sound the soft rustle of the leaves in the garden. Alex stood still, his hands clenched into fists at his sides. The tension in the air was palpable, as if the very ground beneath them was waiting for something to shift, to break.

Finally, Alex spoke, his voice steady but filled with emotion. "Sarah... I don't know what to say. This... this changes everything."

Samantha felt her chest tighten, as if the weight of his words were pressing down on her, suffocating her. She had expected this, expected him to be angry, to feel betrayed. She had built walls for so long, convinced herself that no one could ever truly know her, that no one could ever get close enough to see the truth. But now, she was standing in front of him, vulnerable and exposed, and she didn't know if she could handle the fallout.

"I never wanted this for you," she whispered, her voice trembling. "I never wanted to drag you into my mess."

Alex's gaze softened, and he took a step closer, his hand reaching out to touch hers. "You didn't drag me into anything. I'm here because I care about you, Sarah. I care about the woman you are, not the title you were born into."

Samantha looked up at him, her heart aching with the weight of his words. She wanted to believe him, wanted to believe that he could see past the billionaire's daughter, past the life she had been forced into. But a part of her still held back, still feared that the truth would be too much for him to accept.

"I'm scared, Alex," she said, her voice barely above a whisper. "I don't know if I can live up to the person you think I am. I don't know if I can keep hiding from everything."

Alex squeezed her hand, his touch warm and reassuring. "You don't have to hide anymore, Sarah. Whatever happens, we'll figure it out. Together."

Samantha felt a tear slip down her cheek, but this time, it wasn't out of fear. It was out of something else—something she hadn't allowed herself to feel in years. Hope. She had spent so long running, so long hiding, that she had forgotten what it felt like to truly trust someone, to let them in. But with Alex standing before her, his eyes filled with understanding and compassion, she felt something stir deep within her—a feeling she hadn't allowed herself to feel for so long.

Maybe, just maybe, she could stop running. Maybe she could stop hiding and finally face the truth—not just about her past, but about the future she wanted to build with him.

And for the first time in her life, she felt like the woman she was meant to be.

Seven

The Unraveling

The cool evening breeze swept through the garden, rustling the leaves of the trees and carrying with it the faint scent of jasmine and fresh earth. It should have been peaceful. But for Samantha, the tranquility only deepened the ache that had settled in her chest. The conversation with Alex had left her feeling both liberated and vulnerable, as if she had opened a door to a part of herself she had spent years trying to lock away. But now, she couldn't close it again.

Her mind raced with questions and fears. What would Alex think of her now? Could he accept the truth about who she really was? Her family, her past, everything she had tried so hard to escape—could any of it ever truly be left behind?

The sound of the shop door opening startled her, pulling her from her thoughts. She had been standing in the garden, her hands still dirty from the flowers, the quiet solitude a temporary escape. But the moment she heard the door, she knew exactly who was walking in.

"Sarah," Alex called softly, his voice carrying through the garden. "We need to talk."

She stood frozen, her heart pounding in her chest. She hadn't expected him to come after what had happened, after she had confessed the truth to him. She had expected distance, perhaps anger, maybe even betrayal. But not this. Not his presence here, in this place that had always been hers—her sanctuary.

With a deep breath, she turned and walked toward him. He was standing at the edge of the garden, his eyes searching her face as if he could read every unspoken word. She tried to steady herself, to push down the rising tide of emotions that threatened to overwhelm her.

"I didn't mean to hide anything from you," she said, her voice barely above a whisper. "I just... I didn't know how to tell you."

Alex's expression was unreadable, a mask of calm that only made her feel more exposed. He was too quiet, too still, and it set her on edge. "Sarah, you didn't just hide it," he replied, his tone sharp, though not unkind. "You lied to me. You've been lying to me the whole time."

His words stung more than she had expected, and she felt a knot form in her stomach. She hadn't wanted to lie. She had wanted to protect him from the life she had left behind, to protect herself from the weight of her past, from the legacy she couldn't escape.

"I didn't want you to know," she said, her voice breaking. "I didn't want you to see me for what I really am—a woman trapped by expectations, by wealth, by everything I never asked for."

Alex stepped closer, his gaze steady but piercing. "I know that, Sarah. But it's not just about your family's money. It's about trust. You've kept so many secrets from me, and now I'm left here wondering if I ever really knew you at all. If I ever really knew who you were."

The words hit her like a physical blow, and for a moment, she couldn't breathe. The room felt smaller, the walls closing in as if the world were shrinking around her. She had never allowed herself to be vulnerable—not truly. But with Alex, it had felt so different. She had thought they had something real. She had hoped that they could build something together, something that wasn't defined by her past or her family's wealth. But now, standing before him, the truth felt like an insurmountable barrier between them.

"I didn't mean for it to happen like this," she whispered, the tears welling in her eyes. "I wanted to be someone else here. I wanted to be free."

Alex didn't say anything at first. He just stood there, watching her with an unreadable expression. The silence between them stretched on, suffocating in its weight.

Finally, he spoke, his voice low and full of frustration. "I get it. I do. You're running from something. But you don't have to do it alone, Sarah. I've been here. I've been by your side through all of this. But now, I don't know if I can keep doing this. I don't know if I can keep loving someone who won't even let me see them for who they truly are."

The words hit her like a wave, crashing over her with a force she hadn't anticipated. She had never been good at letting people in, at trusting them with her truth. But now, she was faced with the consequences of her own fear, of her own inability to be honest, even with the one person who had made her feel seen.

"I didn't want to hurt you," she said, her voice cracking. "I never wanted to hurt you, Alex."

He shook his head, taking a step back. "You didn't just hurt me, Sarah. You kept me in the dark. You made me think that what we had was real. And now I'm left here wondering if I was just part of some fantasy you built for yourself."

The words cut deeper than anything else he could have said. The pain of it, the rawness of his disappointment, settled in her chest like a heavy stone. She had never wanted this. She had never wanted to hurt him. But in the process of trying to protect herself, she had pushed him away. She had kept him at arm's length, afraid of what would happen if he knew the truth. And now, she was losing him because of it.

"I'm sorry," she whispered, her voice breaking as the tears began to fall freely. "I never meant to make you feel like that. I just... I didn't know how to let go. How to let you in."

Alex didn't respond immediately. He just stood there, watching her with a look of both sorrow and resignation. "I can't do this anymore, Sarah. I can't keep living in a world where nothing is what it seems. Where I don't even know who I'm really in love with."

His words hit her like a punch to the gut. She opened her mouth to speak, to apologize again, but the words wouldn't come. The truth of what she had done, the reality of her own fears and insecurities, had caught up to her, and now there was nothing she could do to fix it. The walls she had built to protect herself were collapsing, and with them, everything she had tried to create with Alex was falling apart.

"I'm sorry," she whispered again, her voice barely audible. "I never meant for this to happen."

Alex's eyes softened for a moment, but the hardness in his expression remained. "I don't know if I can forgive you for this, Sarah. Not right now. I need time. Time to think. Time to figure out if I can trust you again."

The words were a dagger to her heart. She had never wanted this. She had never wanted to lose him, but in her fear of being known, of being loved for who she really was, she had driven him away.

"I understand," she said softly, her voice filled with defeat. "Take all the time you need. I won't push you. I won't… I won't try to fix this. I'll leave you to figure it out."

Alex nodded, his gaze lingering on her for a moment longer. Then, without another word, he turned and walked away, disappearing into the night, leaving her standing there in the garden, alone.

Samantha sank to her knees, the weight of the moment crashing down on her like a flood. She had lost him. She had lost everything she had worked so hard to build. And as the tears fell freely, she realized that the unraveling had already begun. She had tried to outrun her past, to hide from who she really was. But in doing so, she had lost the only person who had ever truly seen her.

And now, there was no going back.

The garden, once a sanctuary, now felt like a prison. She had built it to escape, but now, all she could do was sit among the flowers and let the truth of her mistakes wash over her. The unraveling had begun, and there was nothing she could do to stop it.

Eight

Fractured Trust

The days after Alex walked away were the longest of Samantha's life. The air around her felt suffocating, heavy with the weight of her choices and the consequences that followed. The world, once so full of color and life, now seemed muted, a blur of shadows and uncertainty. Every corner of the flower shop, every petal she arranged, reminded her of the gaping hole that Alex had left behind. She couldn't escape it. It was there, haunting her, at every turn.

She had always been good at hiding. She had hidden from her family's expectations, from her past, from the world that demanded so much of her. But now, the walls she had carefully built around herself were crumbling, and there was nothing she could do to stop it.

Samantha walked slowly through the shop, her fingers brushing over the rows of flowers she had so lovingly arranged. The once comforting scents now felt cloying, each fragrance a bitter reminder of everything that had gone wrong. The shop, her sanctuary, now felt more like a prison. And it was all her fault.

The door to the shop opened, the soft chime of the bell barely registering in her mind. She didn't even need to look up to know who it was. She could feel the presence before she heard the footsteps—slow, deliberate, and familiar.

"Sarah," Alex's voice came from behind her, low and uncertain.

Her heart skipped a beat, but she didn't turn to face him. She couldn't. She couldn't look him in the eyes after everything that had happened. The guilt, the shame, the fear of losing him forever—it was all too much.

"I didn't expect you to come back," she said, her voice hoarse. She kept her back to him, focusing on a bouquet of daisies in front of her, anything to avoid the piercing gaze she knew he was giving her.

"I don't know what I'm doing here," Alex replied, his voice soft but filled with an undercurrent of frustration. "I didn't know what else to do."

Samantha took a deep breath, forcing herself to keep her emotions in check. "You don't have to do anything, Alex. You made it clear that you needed time. And I understand that."

There was a long pause. She could feel his gaze on her, feel the weight of the unspoken words hanging between them. But she didn't have the strength to say anything more. She had been holding onto hope for so long, but she knew that hope was fragile. It had been built on a lie, a misunderstanding of who she truly was.

"I don't know if I can forgive you," Alex finally said, his voice tight with emotion. "I don't know if I can trust you again."

Samantha's heart dropped, her stomach twisting into a knot. She had expected it. She had known, deep down, that this was coming. But hearing the words, hearing the raw pain in his voice, made it feel real. It was real. She had lost him.

"I know," she whispered. "I don't expect you to forgive me. Not yet. I've done nothing but hurt you, Alex. I lied to you. I kept so much from you, and now… now I don't even know how to fix it."

"I need time," Alex said, his voice tinged with sorrow. "I can't just pretend like everything's fine. You… you were someone else when we first met. And that's not who you are, Sarah. That's not who I fell for."

Samantha felt a sharp pang in her chest. She knew it was true. She had hidden behind the name "Sarah," behind the simple life she had created in Greenvale. She had convinced herself that she could escape, that she could outrun her past. But Alex had seen through it. He had seen the real her, and he had loved her anyway. But now, that love felt like a distant memory, slipping further and further away with each passing moment.

"I'm sorry," she said, her voice barely audible. "I never meant for you to feel like that. I never meant for any of this to happen."

"You've hurt me, Sarah," Alex replied, his tone softening, but still full of pain. "But I think the person you've hurt the most is yourself."

The words hit her like a punch to the gut. It was true. She had spent so much time running from everything—her family, her wealth, the expectations that had been placed on her—she hadn't stopped to think about what she was really running from. She hadn't stopped to think about what she was losing along the way.

"I don't know how to fix this," Samantha whispered, her hands trembling as she clenched the petals of the flowers in front of her. "I don't know how to make it right."

Alex took a step closer, his footsteps hesitant, as if he wasn't sure if he should. "I don't know either," he said quietly. "But I can't keep pretending that everything's fine when it's not. We can't just ignore what's happened, Sarah."

Samantha nodded, feeling the weight of the truth in his words. She had tried to ignore it, to push it aside, to pretend that everything would work out. But now, she couldn't deny it any longer. She had made a mistake. She had broken his trust, and there was no easy way to fix it.

"I think... I think we need some space," Alex said after a long pause, his voice quiet but firm. "I need to figure out if I can trust you again. And you need to figure out what you really want."

Samantha closed her eyes, a single tear slipping down her cheek. The pain of it, the emptiness, the fear that she might never be able to repair the damage she had caused—it was almost too much to bear. She had always believed in control, in hiding behind walls, in keeping herself safe. But now, all those walls had come crashing down, and she was left standing in the rubble, exposed and broken.

"Okay," she whispered, barely able to keep her voice steady. "I understand. I'll give you the space you need. I don't want to push you into anything. I just... I just want you to know that I'm sorry. For everything."

There was a long silence between them, thick with unspoken words and unshed tears. Samantha could feel the distance between them, the gulf that had opened up with her lies and her mistakes. And though part of her wanted to reach out, to try and fix it, she knew it wasn't the right time. Not yet.

Alex nodded, his expression a mix of sadness and resignation. "I need time, Sarah. But I don't know if I can keep living like this. I don't know if I can keep holding on to something that feels broken."

Samantha watched as Alex turned and walked toward the door, each step heavy with finality. As the door clicked shut behind him, she felt her heart shatter into a million pieces. The shop was silent once again, the air thick with the absence of the one person who had made her feel alive, who had made her believe that she could be more than just the sum of her family's expectations.

She sank to the floor, her knees giving way beneath her, and for the first time in years, she allowed herself to feel the weight of everything she had been running from. The truth had caught up with her. And now, there was nothing left but the painful, aching realization that she had lost the one thing that mattered the most.

Her phone buzzed on the counter, but she didn't bother to check it. It could be her father, another reminder of the world she had tried so hard to escape. But she couldn't face it. Not now. Not when the one person who had seen her for who she truly was was walking away.

The garden outside was still beautiful, still full of life. But to Samantha, it felt like a graveyard, a place where dreams went to die. The unraveling had begun, and now, there was no way to stop it.

Nine

Healing Wounds

The days stretched into a suffocating blur, each one bleeding into the next as Samantha continued to walk through the motions of her life. The flower shop, once her sanctuary, had become nothing more than a hollow reminder of the life she had almost built with Alex. The walls, once filled with the gentle hum of conversation and the soft fragrance of blossoms, now felt cold and silent. Every corner, every petal she touched, seemed to mock her with its quiet perfection. It was a world that had been irrevocably altered, and she was left to navigate it alone.

She spent her days tending to the flowers mechanically, her mind replaying the events of the past few weeks like a broken record. She had thought she could escape her past, leave behind the name she had been born into, the expectations that had always loomed over her. She had wanted to be Sarah, the woman who ran a small flower shop in Greenvale, a woman who was loved for who she was—not for her family's wealth or the legacy they had tried to saddle her with. But now, even that simple life seemed beyond her grasp. She had lost the one person who had ever seen her for who she truly was, and the emptiness that had settled in her chest felt unbearable.

Every time she closed her eyes, she saw Alex's face, his expression a mixture of pain and sorrow. The memory of his words echoed in her mind: "I don't know if I can trust you again." The trust that had been so carefully built between them had been shattered, and now it felt like the very foundation of their relationship had crumbled into dust.

She had given him space, just as he had asked. She hadn't called, hadn't tried to contact him, though every part of her had longed to. She had wanted to apologize, to explain herself, to tell him how much she regretted everything, but she knew that the damage had been done. The rift between them felt insurmountable, and the more time passed, the more it seemed like there was no way back.

The shop bell jingled, snapping her from her thoughts. She looked up, startled, as a familiar figure stepped inside, the door creaking softly behind him.

Alex.

Her heart lurched, and for a moment, she couldn't breathe. He was standing there, in front of her, just like before—but everything had changed. His eyes met hers, and she saw something in them that made her chest tighten. It wasn't anger, or even disappointment anymore. It was… uncertainty. It was as though he didn't know where to start, or how to bridge the gap between them.

"Sarah," Alex said quietly, his voice hesitant. "Can we talk?"

She swallowed hard, trying to steady herself. She had no idea what he was going to say, but she knew she needed to hear it. She needed to know if there was any chance, however small, that they could move past everything that had happened.

"Of course," she replied, her voice shaking despite her efforts to remain calm. She gestured toward the small table at the back of the shop. "Sit. Please."

Alex nodded and walked over to the table, his steps slow, measured. Samantha followed him, her heart pounding in her chest. She didn't know what to expect, but she could feel the weight of the moment pressing down on her. This could be the moment when everything changed—or the moment when she lost him for good.

Alex sat down, running a hand through his hair as he looked up at her. There was a vulnerability in his expression, a rawness that made her stomach churn. This wasn't the Alex she had known. This was a man who had been hurt, who was still carrying the weight of everything that had come before.

"I've been thinking a lot," Alex began, his voice quieter now, as if choosing his words carefully. "About us. About everything."

Healing Wounds

Samantha nodded, unable to speak. She didn't know how to fill the silence, didn't know how to make this easier. All she could do was wait, her hands trembling at her sides.

"I've been angry, Sarah. I've been hurt," he continued, his gaze steady. "But the more I think about it, the more I realize… I don't want to lose you. I don't want to lose what we had."

Samantha's heart skipped a beat. The words she had been waiting to hear—I don't want to lose you—came crashing over her, washing away the fear, the doubt, the pain that had been gnawing at her. But even as the relief surged through her, the weight of his next words began to settle in.

"But… I can't pretend like nothing happened," Alex added, his voice tinged with sadness. "I can't just forget the fact that you lied to me, that you kept so much from me. Trust is… it's not something that just comes back overnight."

Samantha felt her chest tighten again. She had known it wouldn't be easy. She had known that trust, once broken, couldn't simply be rebuilt with a few words or promises. But hearing the rawness in his voice, seeing the pain in his eyes, made it all the more real.

"I know," she whispered, her voice thick with emotion. "I know I've hurt you. And I hate myself for it. I never wanted to hurt you, Alex. I never wanted to lie to you. I was just… scared. I was scared that if you knew the truth, you would see me as nothing more than my family's wealth, as nothing more than the life they wanted me to live."

Alex's gaze softened, but the hurt still lingered in his eyes. "I didn't care about the money, Sarah. I never did. What I cared about was you. I cared about the person you were. The person you showed me. But now... I don't know who that person is anymore."

Samantha closed her eyes, the sting of his words piercing her heart. "I'm still that person," she said softly, her voice breaking. "I'm still Sarah, the woman who loves flowers, who loves this town. The woman who was happy for the first time in years. But I've spent so much time pretending, so much time hiding from my past, that I don't even know how to be honest with myself anymore."

There was a long silence between them, thick with the weight of everything unspoken. Samantha's breath caught in her throat as she watched Alex, waiting for him to speak, to say something that would either break her or rebuild her.

"I don't know how to fix this," Alex finally said, his voice barely above a whisper. "I don't know how to heal the trust that's been broken. But I want to try. I want to try to understand you, Sarah. To understand why you did what you did. To understand you."

Samantha felt a surge of hope, though it was fragile and tentative. "I want to try, too," she said, her voice steadying. "I want to try to earn your trust back. I want to show you who I really am, the person you've never had the chance to know."

Alex nodded slowly, his eyes searching hers, as though he was looking for something, something that would tell him she was being honest. "I can't promise you that everything will be fixed overnight. But I'm willing to try. For us."

The words settled between them, and Samantha felt her heart begin to heal, one small crack at a time. It wasn't perfect. It wasn't the happy ending she had dreamed of. But it was a beginning. A fragile, uncertain beginning, but a beginning nonetheless.

As Alex stood to leave, he reached out and took her hand, his grip warm and steady. "We'll take it one day at a time, okay? No more secrets. No more pretending. Just… us."

Samantha nodded, her eyes brimming with tears. "One day at a time," she repeated, the weight of the moment finally beginning to sink in. It wouldn't be easy. There would be moments of doubt, of fear, of old wounds reopening. But in that moment, as they stood in the shop surrounded by the flowers that had always brought her comfort, she knew that she wasn't alone anymore.

And maybe, just maybe, they could rebuild what had been broken. Together.

Ten

Blooming Together

The soft, golden light of dawn filtered through the window, casting a warm glow over the flower shop. The air smelled of fresh blooms, a mixture of lavender, roses, and jasmine, with a hint of earthy undertones. To Samantha, the familiar scent was both a comfort and a reminder of everything that had changed in the past few weeks. The shop, once a peaceful retreat, now felt like a place of reckoning, a place where the past and the future collided, leaving her wondering if she could ever truly escape the weight of her own choices.

She stood behind the counter, her hands moving mechanically as she arranged a bouquet of lilies and daisies. Her mind was a swirl of thoughts—thoughts of Alex, thoughts of her family, and, more than anything, thoughts of the life she had fought so hard to build in Greenvale. The quiet town had given her the peace she had longed for, but now, that peace felt fragile, like a

Blooming Together

delicate petal on the verge of falling.

The door to the shop creaked open, and Samantha's heart skipped a beat. She didn't need to look up to know who it was. She had been expecting him, hoping for him to return, but she wasn't sure what she would say when he did. The last time they had spoken, the trust between them had been shattered, and though they had started to rebuild, she wasn't sure if it would ever be the same.

"Sarah," Alex's voice rang out, and her heart jolted in her chest. It was soft, hesitant, but there was something in it that made her stomach flutter.

She took a deep breath and finally looked up, meeting his eyes. They were filled with a mixture of hope and uncertainty, the same emotions she had seen in him the last time they had spoken. The distance between them had been painful, each passing day a reminder of the brokenness that had been left in the wake of their misunderstanding. But now, as he stood before her, there was something different in his gaze. Something that made her believe that maybe, just maybe, they could start over.

"Alex," she said softly, her voice trembling as she took a step toward him. "I wasn't expecting you."

"I know," he replied, his lips curving into a faint, tentative smile. "I wasn't sure if I was ready to come back, but... here I am."

The words hung in the air between them, the silence thick

with unspoken emotions. They had both been hurt, both been scarred by the lies and secrets, but the truth was—neither of them could walk away from what they had shared. Samantha had tried to convince herself that she could live without him, that her independence was more important than anything else. But deep down, she knew that wasn't true. The connection they shared, the bond that had formed between them, was too strong to ignore.

"Alex, I…" She stopped herself, unsure of how to continue. She had apologized so many times already, but words felt insufficient. She needed more than just an apology. She needed to show him that she was willing to do whatever it took to prove that she was worthy of his trust.

He took a step closer, his eyes softening. "You don't have to apologize anymore, Sarah. We've both made mistakes. I've made mistakes. But I can't keep running from this. From us."

The words caught in her throat, and for a moment, she couldn't find the strength to speak. She had spent so much time hiding from the truth, from the life she had left behind, that she had forgotten what it felt like to be open, to be vulnerable. But now, as she stood in front of him, she realized that this was the only way forward. There was no more hiding, no more pretending. It was time to face everything—together.

Samantha reached out, her hand trembling as she took his. His touch was warm, steady, grounding her in the present. "I don't know what the future holds, Alex," she said quietly, her voice breaking. "But I want to try. I want to rebuild what we had. If you'll let me."

For a moment, Alex didn't respond. He just stood there, holding her hand, his eyes searching hers as though he was looking for something. Then, slowly, he nodded.

"I want that too," he said, his voice full of conviction. "I've been scared, Sarah. Scared that I couldn't trust you again, scared that you wouldn't let me in. But I can't let fear control me anymore. I want to build something real with you. Something that's just ours."

Samantha's heart fluttered in her chest as the words sank in. They were both scared. They had both been hurt. But now, they were standing here, together, willing to try again. It wasn't going to be easy. Trust, once broken, wasn't something that could be easily repaired. But in this moment, with Alex standing before her, she felt something stir within her—hope. A fragile, uncertain hope that maybe, just maybe, they could make it through this. Together.

"Then let's do it," she said softly, her voice full of determination. "Let's take it one step at a time. No more secrets, no more lies. Just us."

Alex's smile widened, and for the first time in what felt like forever, Samantha felt a weight lift from her chest. There was no going back. They had both made mistakes, but they had also chosen to move forward. And that, she realized, was what truly mattered.

The Billionaire's Secret Garden

The sound of the doorbell jingled again, and a familiar figure stepped inside the shop, interrupting the moment between them. Samantha turned to see her father standing in the doorway, his face stern and unyielding. The sight of him sent a ripple of tension through her, and her stomach twisted in knots. She hadn't seen him in weeks, and though she had known this day would come, she wasn't sure if she was ready to face him.

"Sarah," her father's voice was cold, demanding. "I've been looking for you. We need to talk."

Alex immediately stepped forward, his hand still holding Samantha's. "Now's not the time, Mr. McAllister," Alex said firmly, his voice low but filled with authority. "If you have something to say, it can wait."

Her father's eyes flicked toward Alex, narrowing in quiet appraisal. But instead of arguing, he simply stood there, his gaze shifting back to Samantha.

"You've made your choice, then," her father said, his voice a mix of frustration and resignation. "I was hoping you would come to your senses, Sarah. But it seems you've chosen this... small-town life over the family you've been given. Over the legacy you're supposed to uphold."

Samantha's heart pounded in her chest as her father's words echoed in her ears. He had always tried to control her, always tried to force her into the mold he had created for her. But for the first time, as she stood there with Alex beside her, she didn't feel the weight of his expectations crushing her.

"I'm not who you want me to be," she said, her voice steady but filled with finality. "And I don't owe you anything. I've made my own choices now, and I'm living the life I've always wanted. You can't control me anymore."

Her father's gaze flicked from Samantha to Alex, and for a moment, there was an uncomfortable silence. But then, without another word, he turned on his heel and walked out of the shop, his footsteps echoing in the quiet space.

As the door closed behind him, Samantha let out a breath she hadn't realized she was holding. The tension that had gripped her for so long began to loosen, and she realized that this was the first time in her life that she had truly stood up for herself. She had chosen her own path. She had chosen Alex.

"You're not alone anymore," Alex said quietly, his voice warm and reassuring. "We'll face this together."

Samantha turned to look at him, her heart full as she realized just how much she had been holding on to—the fears, the guilt, the expectations. And now, with Alex by her side, she was ready to let it all go.

"I'm not alone," she whispered, her voice thick with emotion. "And for the first time, I'm not running away from who I am. I'm not running away from us."

They stood hand in hand as the sun began to set outside the window, casting a golden light over the shop. The future was still uncertain and filled with challenges, but for the first time in a long time, Samantha felt hopeful. There would be struggles, no doubt, but she wasn't facing them alone.

Together, they would rebuild, bloom, and this time, do it on their own terms.

www.ingramcontent.com/pod-product-compliance
Lightning Source LLC
LaVergne TN
LVHW020435080526
838202LV00055B/5206